Two at the Zoo

Holly Smith Dinbergs

illustrated by

Monika Maddock

MACMILLAN

First published in 2008 by
MACMILLAN EDUCATION AUSTRALIA PTY LTD
15–19 Claremont Street, South Yarra 3141

Visit our website at www.macmillan.com.au or
go directly to www.macmillanlibrary.com.au

Associated companies and representatives throughout the world.

National Library of Australia
Cataloguing-in-Publication data

Smith Dinbergs, Holly.
Two at the zoo.

For primary school students.
ISBN 978 1 4202 6142 4 (pbk.).
ISBN 978 1420262179 (set 3)

1. Zoos – Juvenile fiction. I. Title. (Series: Girlz rock!).

A 823.4

Series created by Felice Arena and Phil Kettle
Project management by Limelight Publishing Services Pty Ltd
Cover and text design by Lore Foye
Illustrations by Monika Maddock

Printed in China

GIRLZ ROCK!

Contents

Jules *Rosa*

CHAPTER 1

Where'd They Go?

Best friends Jules and Rosa are on a special trip with their class.

Rosa "Jules, who am I? Guess."

Rosa starts walking in a circle, taking huge steps and pounding on her chest.

Jules “Hmmm … someone who’s crazy?”

Rosa “No way. Try again.”

She continues walking and pounding. Then she begins to growl.

Jules “Frankenstein?”

Rosa “Wrong! Here’s a clue. Where are we?”

She points to the sign above their head that says “ZOO”.

Jules (shrugging) “So we’re at the zoo. That doesn’t help. I give up. Who are ya?”

Rosa “C’mon, it’s so obvious. I’m King Kong. Don’t ya see?”

Jules (laughing) "Maybe more like his little sister. What was her name? Oh yeah, Ding Dong."

Jules and Rosa stand at the back of the group. Their teacher, Miss Walker, has told the students to stay with the group at all times.

Jules "I can't wait to see the gorillas. What do you wanna see?"

Rosa "Hmmmm ... the monkeys ... and the giraffes ... and the koalas. Oh, and the bears."

Jules "You wanna see everything."

Rosa (excited) "Look—baby lions! They are sooooo cute."

Jules "Chill, Ro. That's only a poster."

The girls stop to admire a huge poster with pictures of baby lions, until Jules looks up.

Jules "Do you hear that?"
Rosa "I don't hear anything."
Jules "That's the point. It's too quiet. Where'd everybody go?"

Rosa (shocked) "They left without us."

Jules "Miss Walker's gonna be mad. We'd better find 'em."

Rosa "Hurry!"

The girls run down the path, looking for their classmates.

CHAPTER 2

Major Poo

The girls arrive at a clearing where several paths intersect. They see a sign with arrows pointing in different directions, showing people where to go to see monkeys, alligators, lions, elephants and tigers. No Miss Walker, and no classmates.

Jules “Now what? Call the police? That’s what Mum says to do if I get lost.”

Rosa “Call who? The zoo police? They’ll probably lock us up in a big cage.”

Jules “With the baby lions? Cool!”

Rosa “Jules, think! Where can we find them?”

Jules "Didn't Miss Walker say something about elephants?"

Rosa "Yeah. She said we were gonna start with the elephants."

Jules "Elephants are that way."

The girls follow the arrow towards the elephants.

Rosa "Smell that?"

Jules wrinkles her nose, making a face.

Jules "What stinks?"

Rosa "Whew! That's what I call a major pile of poo."

The girls come to a large fence through which they see a herd of elephants.

Rosa "That little one is soooooo cute. Do you think it's a girl or a boy elephant?"

Jules "Do I look like a vet?"

Rosa "That's what I'm going to be when I grow up. Did I tell ya?"

Jules (groaning) "Only about a gazillion times."

The baby elephant puts up its trunk and sprays water right at the girls.

Rosa "She wants to play."

Jules "No time, Rosa. Gotta find our class."

Rosa "You're right. Which way?"

Jules "That way."

The girls choose a new path and run down it. A moment later, the girls stop short—eyes wide open and scared!

CHAPTER 3

Roar!

Jules and Rosa are face to face with a roaring tiger.

Jules (scared) "That mouth! Those teeth! He could swallow us whole. Rosa, run for it!"

Rosa (calmly) "No worries."

Jules "Are you crazy? You wanna die?"

Rosa "Jules, did ya notice that we're looking through a big window?"

Jules "Huh?"

Jules reaches out and touches the window. The girls notice the sign under the window, showing the tiger's name.

Rosa "Jules, meet Claudio."

Jules (embarrassed) "Oh ... it looks like he's standing right next to us."

The tiger roars again. Jules puts her hands over her ears.

Jules "Yikes! Claudio is really loud."

Rosa "I think he's really mad."

Jules "Maybe he was sleeping and we woke him up."

Rosa "Hmmm ... I don't think so."

Jules "Maybe he has a toothache. With those fangs, he must have a toothbrush as big as me."

Rosa "Do ya see how he keeps licking his paw? I think he's hurt."

Jules "Not much we can do about that now. C'mon. We gotta go. Miss Walker's looking for us."

Rosa turns and, with hands on hips, looks at her friend.

Rosa "Are you telling me that, if I were hurt, you wouldn't try to help me?"

Jules "Course I would. But you don't have gigantic teeth and like to eat people for snacks. Ro, his paw is bigger than my head."

Rosa "There's gotta be something that we can do to help."

Jules "You're not a vet yet. There's nothing we can do."

Rosa "Oh, yes there is."

CHAPTER 4

Dr. Ro to the Rescue

A young woman dressed in a zookeeper's uniform is entering the little building next to the tiger enclosure. Rosa runs over and talks to her, and then comes back to join Jules.

Jules "Who was that?"

Rosa "That's Claudio's keeper."

Jules "What did you tell her?"

Rosa "That he's upset 'cause he has a hurt paw. She's gonna take a look."

Jules "She's not afraid?"

Rosa "Afraid of what?"

Jules "Afraid of winding up as Claudio's lunch?"

Rosa "She's only gonna look. I guess she'll call the vet if she has to."

The girls watch through the window as the keeper studies Claudio from the other side of a steel gate. A few minutes later, she takes a mobile phone from her pocket and makes a call.

Jules "Who's she calling?"
Rosa "Who d'ya think?"
Jules "The tiger's mummy?"

Rosa rolls her eyes.

Jules “Wait, I know—an ambulance, to take him to the Emergency Room.”

The keeper leaves the building next to the tiger enclosure. She walks over and tells Rosa that the vet is going to visit Claudio, and, thanks to Rosa, he should be okay.

Jules "Good work, Dr. Ro. Let's go. Maybe we can find the class before Miss Walker even notices that we're gone."

The girls turn to leave. Suddenly, they come face to face with a frowning Miss Walker.

CHAPTER 5

Rock Star

Miss Walker talks to the girls to find out what happened to them, and then leads them back to join the group.

Rosa “I’m sure glad Miss Walker wasn’t too mad at us.”

Jules "How could she be mad? You saved Claudio. You should get a medal."

Rosa stops and stares at her friend.

Rosa "A medal? Me? Really?"

Jules "Totally. There should be a ceremony, just like the Olympics. Just think—you step up on a box, then some really important person gives you a medal. A gold one."

Rosa "Who's this really important person who's gonna give me a medal?"

Jules "Who do you think? Me, of course."

Rosa smiles as she imagines Jules presenting her with a gold medal.

Rosa "There should be music. They always play really loud music when somebody wins a medal."

Miss Walker waves at the girls, so they begin walking again, trying to catch up to the class.

Jules "You are so right. We need music. And, I know just who should play."

Rosa "Who?"

Jules "The music should come from your new best friend."

Rosa "Huh? Sometimes I have no idea what you're talking about."

Jules "You know. Your new favourite rock group."

Rosa "I have a new favourite rock group?"

Jules "I'm talking about Claudio. With that name, he could be a rock star."

Rosa (laughing) "And the name of his group is ...?"

Jules "The Sore Paws?"

Rosa "The Terrible Tigers?"

Jules "I got it—The Fangs! That's a cool name for a group. Especially if it's a group of tigers."

Miss Walker tells the class in a loud voice to follow her to the next stop.

Rosa "Cool! The Monkey House."

Jules "Great, Ding Dong. Maybe we'll see your big, hairy brother."

Jules

GIRLZROCK!

Zoo Lingo

Rosa

"Code One" What zookeepers yell if there is a dangerous animal on the loose!

endangered animal An animal that's in danger of disappearing entirely. If animals are endangered, they need to be protected, or they will become extinct and totally disappear from the Earth.

gift shop Where you can go at the end of your trip to the zoo to buy cool stuff like an elephant key chain for your friend or a tiger pin for your mum.

keeper Someone who takes care of the animals every day. Keepers do different tasks like feeding animals and picking up poo.

veterinary surgeon A doctor who takes care of animals only.

GiRLZROCK!

Zoo Must-dos

☆ Never try to pat a tiger, or any other wild animal, no matter how cute and cuddly they look.

☆ Get used to the idea of picking up poo if you want to work around animals.

☆ If it's a sunny day, make sure you have a cool pair of sunglasses and a hat when you go to the zoo.

☆ Wear something with orange and black stripes if you're having lunch with a group of tigers. That way, you'll fit right in. (But make sure that you don't wind up as the lunch.)

☆ Start studying if you want to work in a zoo. Most zoo jobs require a university degree.

☆ Before you go to the zoo, make a list of the animals you absolutely positively have to see during your visit. That way, you won't miss out on your favourites!

☆ Don't feed wild animals anything they shouldn't eat (like your favourite lollies)! It could be really dangerous for them.

☆ If you work as a tiger or lion keeper, follow all the safety rules to prevent yourself or anybody else from becoming a cat snack!

Zoo Instant Info

- There are lots of great websites with information about the zoos of the world. You can even see live webcams of different animals!
- Zoos are designed with three groups in mind: animals, keepers and visitors, like you and your friends.
- Many zoos let you adopt an animal (like a tiger or a baby elephant). When you adopt an animal, you give money to help pay for its care and feeding, but it doesn't come to live in your home.
- Zoo jobs are hard to get, because they are so popular. If you want to get a job in a zoo, you need to know a lot about science (at least a university degree) and you need lots of experience working with animals.

- Animals that are sick go to the animal doctor, called the veterinary surgeon (or "vet" for short). Vets figure out what the problem is and treat it. Vets also give the animals regular check-ups to catch problems early, so that they stay healthy.
- Animal care managers manage groups of animals, such as birds or reptiles. Keepers take care of individual animals on a day-to-day basis.
- Zoo curators decide which animals to bring into the zoo and which animals should visit, or be traded to, another zoo.
- There are good zoo jobs for people who don't want to work directly with animals. Zoos need people to keep the machines running, manage the money and work in the gift shop.

GIRLZ ROCK!

Think Tank

1 What kind of animals should you never try to pat?

2 What should you wear if you're having lunch with a bunch of tigers?

3 If you can't get to the zoo, but you want to see some wild animals, what should you do?

4 When can you feed your favourite lollies to wild animals?

5 Is it easy or hard to get a job at the zoo?

6 What do you do if you're at the zoo and you hear one of the keepers yell "Code One"?

7 Where do sick animals go?

8 What do most people do when they work at the zoo?

Answers

1 You should never try to pat wild animals.

2 If you're having lunch with a bunch of tigers, make sure to wear something with orange and black stripes—that way you'll blend in.

3 If you can't get to a zoo, ask your mum or dad if they can help you find a live webcam so that you can see some wild animals in a zoo somewhere in the world.

4 Never feed a wild animal lollies. It might be dangerous!

5 It's hard to get a job at the zoo—you often need a university degree and lots of experience working with animals.

6 If you're at the zoo, and you hear a keeper yell "Code One", look out! That means a dangerous animal is on the loose.

7 Sick animals go to the veterinary surgeon.

8 Most people who work at the zoo have to pick up a lot of poo!

How did you score?

- If you got all 8 answers correct, start studying to become a vet so that you can work full time at the zoo with the animals you love!
- If you got 6 answers correct, think about a career managing the gift shop at the zoo, so that you get a discount on cool animal key chains for all your friends.
- If you got fewer than 4 answers correct, practise picking up poo so that one day you can volunteer at a zoo.

Hey Girls!

I hope you had fun reading this story. You know what I love most about reading? I can open a book and read a fantastic story about funny people or cool animals without even moving. And I can read wherever I want—in my room, in the library, in the park—anywhere. (When I was little, I tried to read in the car, but it made me feel sick. If that happens to you, ask your mum or dad about using some headphones to listen to books recorded on CDs.)

You can have even more fun if you read "Two at the Zoo" out loud with somebody else—like your best friend or mum or dad. Here's another idea—you and your class can use this story to put on a play.

To bring the story to life, get some cool props. What would work for this story? A poster of baby lions? A stuffed elephant? A tiger puppet?

Who will be Jules? Who will be Rosa? Who will be the narrator? (That's the person who reads the parts between Jules and Rosa.) Maybe a talent scout will visit your class and you'll be invited to Hollywood for a movie audition. No matter what happens, you'll have fun!

You know what my dad used to tell me? Readers are leaders. So keep reading!

And, always remember—Boyz may think they rule, but Girlz Rock!

Girlz Rock!

When We Were Kids

Holly

Shey

Holly talked to Shey, another *Girlz Rock!* author.

Shey "Did you go to the zoo a lot when you were little?"

Holly "Yes, I used to go to a huge zoo near where I lived. It was fantastic. I especially loved the tigers and lions."

Shey "Were you afraid of them?"

Holly "Well, I remember wondering what would happen if I accidentally fell over the fence and into the tiger area."

Shey "What did you think would happen?"

Holly "That the tiger would be really happy to get a Holly-burger, but that my parents would be really mad at me!"

GIRLZROCK!

What a Laugh!

Q What is orange and black and bounces?

A A tiger on a trampoline!

GIRLZROCK!

Read about the fun that girls have in these GIRLZROCK! titles:

Birthday Party Bedlam

Pony Club

Doubles Trouble

Soccer Crazy

Dance Fever

Minigolf Face-off

Trapeze Dreams

Two at the Zoo

... and 20 more great titles to choose from!